Kitchen Science

Learn about different kinds of food and how to find science in the kitchen.

by Carole Wilkinson

ETA® Cuisenaire

800-445-5985
www.etacuisenaire.com

Kitchen Science
ISBN 0-7406-4155-7
ETA 383161

ETA/Cuisenaire • Vernon Hills, IL 60061-1862
800-445-5985 • www.etacuisenaire.com

Series © 2006 by ETA/Cuisenaire®

Original version published by Nelson Australia Pty Limited (2002).
This edition is published by arrangement with Thomson Learning
Australia.

ETA/Cuisenaire
Manager of Product Development: Mary Watanabe
Creative Services Manager: Barry Daniel Petersen
Production Manager: Jeanette Pletsch
Lead Editor: Betty Hey
Copy Editor: Barbara Wrobel
Production Artist: Diana Chiropolos
Graphic Designer: Amy Endlich

Photographs by Fotograffiti
Illustrations on pp. iii, 2, 8, 16, 18, and 28 by Vasja Koman

Teacher consultant: Garry Chapman, Ivanhoe Grammar School

Printed in China.

06 07 08 09 10 11 12 13 14 15   10 9 8 7 6 5 4 3 2 1

Contents

Chapter One

Why Cook?

uncooked spaghetti

cooked spaghetti

When we cook food, it changes. Food can get softer and easier to chew when it's cooked. It often tastes better. Sometimes it changes color. Sometimes it gets bigger or smaller. It's like magic!

Cooking isn't magic, though. When we cook foods, we make them very hot. It is the heat that changes the way food looks and tastes.

Uncooked Starch

Potatoes contain a **chemical** [KEH-mi-kul] called starch. Starch is a white, tasteless substance found in some foods.

uncooked potato

cooked potato

Cooked Starch

When we cook potatoes, the starch grains fill with water and swell.

If we cook the potatoes longer, the starch grains burst. Then the potatoes become soft and tasty.

3

Flour also contains starch. We use different types of flour to thicken sauces, such as custard sauce or gravy.

Stage 1: Add liquid to the flour. The sauce is very thin at this stage.

Stage 2: When the starch grains swell, the sauce thickens.

Stage 3: When the starch grains burst, the sauce gets even thicker.

Fruit and vegetables contain **cellulose** [SELL-you-lows], and those that are hard and crunchy contain a lot of cellulose. Cooking softens the cellulose.

raw carrot

cooked carrot

raw tomato

cooked tomato

raw spinach

cooked spinach

Different foods need to be cooked at different temperatures. Eggs need only low temperatures when they are cooked in water. To cook pizza, though, a restaurant oven has to be very hot.

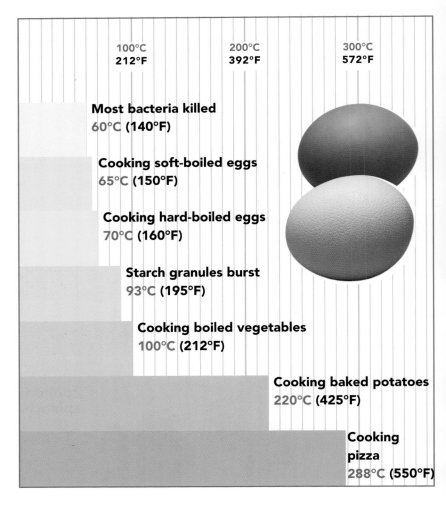

100°C
212°F

200°C
392°F

300°C
572°F

Most bacteria killed
60°C (140°F)

Cooking soft-boiled eggs
65°C (150°F)

Cooking hard-boiled eggs
70°C (160°F)

Starch granules burst
93°C (195°F)

Cooking boiled vegetables
100°C (212°F)

Cooking baked potatoes
220°C (425°F)

Cooking pizza
288°C (550°F)

uncooked chicken

cooked chicken

We don't only cook food to make it taste good and easy to chew. The heat of cooking also kills tiny **microorganisms** in the food. This makes the food safe to eat.

7

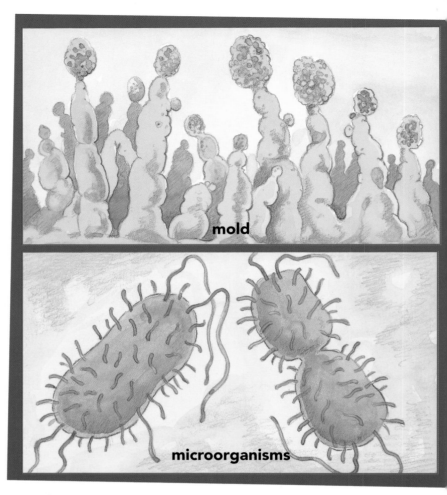

mold

microorganisms

Some microorganisms are tiny creatures that we call **bacteria** [bak-TEER-ee-ah], or germs. They can make you sick.

Other types of microorganisms are tiny plants that we call mold. Cooking our food kills both types of microorganisms.

Chapter Two

All Hot Air

Bread is a very simple food made mostly of flour, water, and yeast. When you mix the ingredients, they become a soft paste called dough [DOE]. If you taste dough, it is gluey and not good to eat.

Air is added to flour
when sifting.

To make bread lighter, bubbles of air and other gases are added.

Bread recipes tell you to sift the flour. This isn't just to get the lumps out. The main reason is to mix it with air.

This yeast is overflowing its container because there are so many gas bubbles.

Another way to make gas is to add yeast to the dough. Yeast is another type of microorganism—a useful one.

We mix yeast with a little sugar and warm water before adding it to the dough.

Place the uncooked dough into a pan where it will rise.

rising dough

The yeast splits the sugar into **alcohol** and a gas called **carbon dioxide**. If we put the dough somewhere warm, the gas makes small bubbles in the dough. The bubbles make the dough grow bigger. This is why bread dough rises.

In the oven, the dough gets very hot.
The high heat eventually kills the yeast.
The bread stops rising and forms a crust.

The shapes of the gas bubbles stay inside the bread and make it soft, spongy, and delicious to eat.

Chapter Three

Exceptional Eggs

egg white

egg yolk

small pocket
of air

Eggs are very useful. They are used in
sweets, such as cakes, pies, and cookies.
They are also used in such foods as omelets.
Inside an egg, there are three parts—the
white, the yolk, and a small pocket of air.

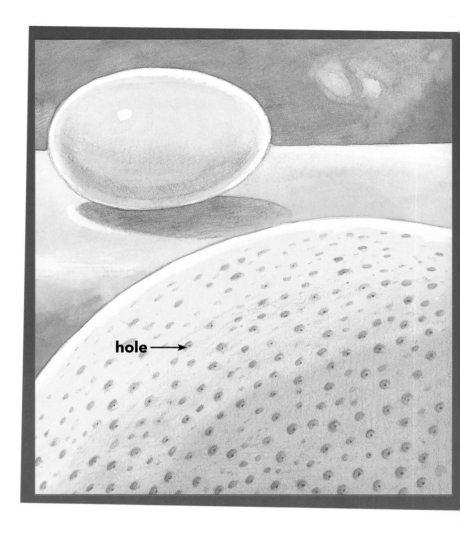

hole ⟶

You can't see them, but an eggshell has thousands and thousands of tiny holes in it. As the egg gets older, air enters the tiny holes and the air pocket inside the egg gets bigger.

16

How Fresh Is Your Egg?

The egg white and the egg yolk contain all the nutrition. But the air pocket is useful, too. It tells us if the egg is fresh. Here's how to find out. Fill a bowl with cold water. Place the egg in it.

If the egg lies on the bottom, it is very fresh. If it stands on the bottom with its big end up, it is not fresh but still okay to eat. If it floats on the top, it is rotten. Throw it away!

Which Egg Is Which?

What happens if you boil some eggs and they get mixed up with the uncooked eggs in the fridge? They all look the same!

Here is a trick for telling them apart.

spin egg

Step 1: Lay the egg on the kitchen counter and spin it around.

Step 2: Stop it from spinning with your finger.

Step 3: Now quickly lift your finger. If the egg is cooked, it will stay still. If it is raw, it will spin a little more.

Chapter Four

Colors in the Kitchen

cabbage

beet

strawberries

Red fruits and vegetables, such as strawberries and beets, contain a chemical that gives them their red color. Red cabbage has lots of this special chemical. Try this experiment using red cabbage and water.

21

1

2

sieve

3

4

Step 1: Chop some red cabbage into thin pieces. Chop enough to fill a jar.

Step 2: Cover the cabbage with boiling water. Leave for half an hour.

Step 3: Pour the mixture through a sieve.

Step 4: Throw away the cabbage and pour the purple water into a small jar.

Step 5: Squeeze some lemon juice into the jar.

Step 6: The liquid turns bright pink. The chemical in the cabbage water turns pink when you add an **acid** such as lemon juice.

Step 7: Empty the jar and rinse it in clean water. Put some more purple cabbage water into the clean jar.

Step 8: Add a teaspoon of baking soda. The liquid turns blue. The chemical in the cabbage water turns blue when you add baking soda.

You should never eat green potatoes as they could make you sick.

Potatoes sometimes change color. It has nothing to do with cooking, though.

Potatoes grow underground. Potatoes exposed to sunlight can make chlorophyll, the chemical that makes plants green. The chlorophyll is harmless, but it is a sign that a bitter substance called solanine has also formed in the green areas.

25

bruised
apple

If you drop an apple, it gets bruised and the part of the apple that gets hit becomes damaged. Air reacts with the damaged apple and a brown chemical called melanin is formed. In apples, this damage will increase decay.

But in raisins, dates, and figs, melanin occurs naturally and gives these fruits their brown color.

This is just some of the science that can be found in your kitchen. What a lot of things to learn! But there is one thing that's easy to remember—food tastes really good, too!

Glossary

acid a sour-tasting liquid

alcohol a colorless, flammable liquid

bacteria [bak-TEER-ee-ah] tiny living bodies that can cause disease

carbon dioxide a colorless, odorless gas

cellulose material that forms the cell walls of plants

chemical [KEH-mi-kul] what something is composed of

microorganisms tiny, single-celled life forms

Index